*The reasons of all my love
My werewolf Kiara*

# Contents

# Bouquet to my grave

I love to get flowers everyday
And who wouldn't?

Feels special, wanted and loved!
Lately, I get them every day.
Since I stopped talking to them in May

They didn't like when I talked
Didn't bother when I was near about
I got no gifts even on my birthdays
I went unnoticed on several days
It all hurt me a lot
I had no option for I loved them all
Till I could…
But now
They've changed
Still I feel nothing.

# Just us!

There is more to love
Than just lust
There is more to life
Than just trust
There is more to me than just us
There is more to live
Than just fuss

# Let me breeze you

I'll become wind
When I die
I the cool autumn wind
I'll sit on your roof and fly
You'll be my sun
When you die
Much above
Where I can't fly
You'll shine on me
Give me warmth
Be with me
Wherever I stalk

# Sully lies

We invented light
Coz we are scared

We live in groups
Coz we hate being alone

We close our eyes at night
Coz we are afraid of the dark

We make noise and speak loud
To hide the silent truth

The truth that we all know
Yet never dare to accept

What truth?
I don't know!

Then, why do I keep
All the lights on

I turn on the TV loud
I'm scared to walk alone
On the dark cemented road
Covered by huge leafy trees
I yearn company

# Of other humans

# Perfection my prey

I'm driving my night out
Midnight in cars
Peaceful roads, no lights
Serene Music of my soul
Unheard, untouched
No – don't touch me
And listen
Listen to our heart beats
Our breath clash
Our fingertips just a spec away
Feel
Feel the flow
From me to you
You to the wind
Cold and wild
Like my hair – unkept and free
Like my dreams
Eccentric and whimsical
Yet mine
So dear to me
So just stay
Stay with me and play
And sway
Sway as you play
The game of love

To pretend to love
When you don't
To pretend to be mine
When you won't
Just stay…
My vampire dairies
My memories of being a geisha
My Chinese bamboo life
My – ME – Mine!
The night
Has risen the devil in me
Again
To hunt
To kill
To suffice
The hunger of a higher
Intellect
The night is my blood

# Daughter of me!

Her heartbeat / she sucks
I feel on my chest/ my breast, without any rest
Love the smell
Of her breath – Unforgettable till death
She can feel me cry
Without any tone
She the queen of my heart
My heart her throne
Million times in a day
I love you she'll say
"A miss you" card daily
With a flowers so gaily
On her knee she'll sit
Unbothered by the world – her wit
With pride she gives – divine love still lives
Love of two woman
Ugly? How can it even be?
Every female is beautiful
By herself just see
Mother in me
Daughter in thee
Love is love, just let it be
Why can't you see, normal it can be
Me holding her hand

In a world that's free

# Imagination? Ghost? Or my fantasy?

Lying on my bed
Listening to carcass music
My heart beating loud
With the rhythm of the clock
Going tick… tick… tick
My mind leaves my body
Opening the window
Fly's out away
Out in the open air
Free in the pouring rain!
I hear no more music
Heart as if stopped! Beats no more
The dead clock
Ticking no where
My soul relishes the freedom;
The fresh evening autumn breeze
I swim up above to the sky
To the grey cotton rolls
Stretching out on the softness
Watching the earth below
Small buildings, small roads
A small sleeping I!
To my left, far at horizon

The sun has gone
And the twilight about to set in
My cushion slowly melting
I search for my wings
OH they are gone!
The cloud has rained
I'm falling down
I grasp the air, I grasp the wind
I grasp my life that's left within
Oh God! I am falling! Help me out!
The land is nearing as I shout
Through the window I see me sleeping
Boldly! I stretch out
Got hold of a strong branch no doubt
Oops! It breaks and I have a fall
I crash to the ground messed all
Open my eyes and see
I'm alright; must be a dream to be
Just tumbled out of bed
It was a lovely dream as I said!
As I sit here writing this down
I hear someone frown
I see myself waving at me
There sitting and smiling from the tree!
Oh my God! What could it be?

# Nights through my window pane

Love city at night
The muted drill
King of the roads
Master of the game
Calm quiet, peaceful
Thrill, chill pill
No sun, pure fun
Wind, breeze, freeze
Tomato sauce with cheese
Love as you please
Silent, secret but serene
Sex in the city

# Huggy Puggy!

At times I wish
I could hug you often
Hug you when I'm happy
Hug you I'm sad
Hug you when I'm Furious
Hug you when I'm Mad
Hug you when I'm Life's perfect
Hug you when I'm Life's bad
Hug you as a lover
Hug you as my dad
Hug you when I feel pathetic
Hug you when I'm glad
Hug you Just to feel you
Hug you as a friend
Hug you as a handsome lad
At times I wish
I could simply hug
As long as I can!

# Reeking love

Sniffing oneself to wonder
What do I stink of!!!

Sweat, sex, cigarette or weed
Tea, tobacco, talc or blood
What possibly could it be?
A mixture – Deadly dangerous
Poison Ivy
Which one, out of the three!
Either of them all
One me!
Hungry, Tasty, nasty, beauty
Me for all
All for me

# Games we play

Centuries lived together,
Still we are so unknown
Words, feeling alive forever
The days now gone, the time blown
Here we walk, as sweet strangers
So very easy, to speak empty words
Every time, our eyes they meet
The invisible tears rolling down your cheek
Will be, will be, whatever it may
The games we play, the games we play!

That cold smile, the piercing words
All dreams shattered dead they lay
Like poor old bride
In cold winter waiting for May
For the love, the lovely game
Thank you, for we lost it again
For the time, friends and fame
All are gone, leaving just pain
Will be, will be, whatever it may
The games we play, the games we play!

# Spring of the unknown

Ideas make
Ideas break
As softly all hearts ache
Diamonds fake;
Like swan lake
Glimmer loud in sun's blache!
All I say are few word
Quite a stupid like sheep's head
At times beautiful like flying bird
Or sour like old curd
Men are made
Men break
It thunders when souls shake
With diamond fake
When dynasties are made
Humanity cries Nature aches
They come, they go
still I don't know
Of irrationality show
Where leads the flow…

# The fall

It's so warm outside
Yet I'm freezing
Your lips, your touch
So pleasing
Muffler wrapped around
Yet I'm cold
Hold on to me now
I'm falling

# Strawberry

On a cold freezing afternoon
Locked up in my room
My lungs filling up with aroma
Of strawberry sauce – drama

The dramatic end of my strawberry sauce
Missing you – my ultimate loss
Strange how strawberry resembles your lips
And your pink nailed finger tips

Soft, mushy and supple
We could have made a great couple…
The little puppy we took home,
Texting for hours on phone

The lake, the rain, the kiss
Oh! How much everything I miss
Starlite night
Smoky and bright

Amazing evening and catching the train
How I cried for you in vain
You were there and you are here
It was my foolish fear

Thinking that I lost you
Actually I never found you
For I never looked in my heart
Where you were from the start!

# *Silent screams*

The less I speak, the more I understand;
The trivialities of life
This very human world we live in
Useless important stuff!
We talk without the need of it
We speak!
We shout!
Scream!
When silence can do it all
Silence with a smile

I stand there silently smiling and the screaming
world shuts up to my sound

# Never ending drama

This smell; the scent; the scenes
Eyes closed, mouth open
Bodies colliding in dreams...
She strips of her black net panties,
His scent fills the washroom
She tries hard to control her tears
But they roll down her
Pink cheeks
The red lips,
Half bitten; half torn
Like lost of love forlorn
Yet they dare to smile
In memories sweet
Of the yet another sinister sin

# He mother!

She is just like me
Or should I say she is me!
Just younger; smarter and a prettier version of me!
I see her talk to him; about her day
And I wonder how come we never discuss those topics;
Just to realize I am the man here
And he is the wife;
So the motherly concern and pampering

# Be up and doing

Just be up and doing
Sure there is lots of trouble
Sure there is heaps of care
Burden that bends us double
Worries that come to wear
We must keep pursuing
Something and see it through
Still to be up and doing
Is all that there is to do
Though you would like to idle
Wait for the world to right
Keep your hand on the bridle
Fight when you have to fight
Woman are won by wooing
Fortune is won the same
And to be up and doing
Is all there is to the game
Fever ever fail by trying
Few win who wait
All of your sitting, singing
Never will conquer fate
Whatever path you're having
One thing is certain, son;
Either be up doing

Or you will end up down and done

# Inner silence and the chirping swap

When the city sleeps
The swamp wakes
From its slumber
The slumber that lasted
The whole day long
Or the party
Unheard in the traffic noise

By twilight
The crickets/ the alarm clocks
Start waking up
Their buzzing heard
Distinct even under
Peak hour traffic

Change of shift
After the bell
The swamp – awake
Crows to hell
Time for them
To go to bed and

Leave the swamp alone

The real beauty
Of the swamp
Is heard in a
Midnight downpour
That lasts
All night long
So does their party

# Mother of love

They just won't understand
They can't even see
I know they all are
Blind; deaf and dumb
She replied

They know nothing
They haven't seen the world
He continued
His frustration
Piling up
But we know
She smiled as she kissed
His forehead
He lay his heavy head
On her soft bosoms
With a sigh
Hugging her tightly
As their souls melted into one…
From
The son of another mother

# The mother of another child

# Magic of Life

Am I being used?
Is the bulb really fused?

The fly high
Word does mean

When we dream
Why not become one

Questions need no answer
For they trap us down

Turning to look into the mirror
She left me haunted

For the invisible to become visible
Just hug me tight

You will learn to disappear
She breathed into him

# Canvas of memory

We have thoughts
That we paint into dreams
Expressing pain to feel it
While the pleasure just leaves
Once you reach through
Stay along and you will
Be the dream, the art, the soul and life

# Sun in the monsoon

The food that feed me

The hunger that garners me

The forgotten thoughts of ambition

Misused to pin down the nighty knight dreams

Dream big my queen

You warrior of light

Shining bright with your smile

Fill the hearts around with life

Make my blood run lost

In the vast wonderland of yours

Sleep in the peace you give me

For the starry nights are just gonna shower soon.

# Birth with burst

Let's find ways to create
The beauty of the darker self;
Experience all the possibility
See the light in it
Absorb the darkness
For it can remain our shadow
Just to destroy it
And start anew
Don't you realize,
We don't sleep anymore
We are born anew everyday
My baby keep smiling

# Winter dream of a peahen

I want to, feel your heartbeats at my lips

I want to, taste your neck with my tongue

I want to, whisper nothing in your ear

I want to; drown in the fragrance of your breath

I want to; kiss the tear at your eyelashes

I want your lips at my soul

I want your fingertips play on my back

I want to rock like a baby in your arms

I want to laugh out loud as you lift me high

I want to quiver as you suck my toe

I want to cry with you as we make love

I want -

You!

# Act of hearing

Seriously
I do listen to just reply
Rather than to understand
I need to talk
To be heard first
Rather than listen empathically
Omg! Seriously!

# Friendly light

You are like the lighthouse

My friend

Each time I get lost

Distracted or hopeless

I know you will

Find me, get me back on track

Motivate me

I may slow down; get tired; rest a while

But you are always in

My sight and mind

My lighthouse – divine!

# *Vanilla creams*

Silent dreams
Of wild nights
Hunger screams
Of sensuous plights
Vanilla creams
Strawberry lights
Unleashed reams
Vertical flights
Sparkling beams
Neon lights
Whispered screams
In disco lights.

# Elasticity of attraction

Are we seriously tied?

With some invisible elastic bands?

The more you push me

The more I keep coming on you

The greater the force

The faster the speed

Invisible it is...

The more I want to go unnoticed

The more I disappear

The more you keep bringing

Me back to life

I run, you follow

A three legged race

You push, I fall

I run, you run

You north and me south

And still we end up

One on one

An ecstatic smooch

A wonderful hug

All invisible

Just like your love!

# Truly deeply madly

Everyone does it

Once in a lifetime

Admit it

You did it too

Here it goes


'See you tomorrow'

She said

To no one in particular

Yet my heart skipped a beat

Her naughty smile

Those glittering eyes

I couldn't sleep all night


Practicing how do I start?

That first impression!

Gotta, nail it

Stupid friends and their

Wild ideas

Cool hunk, book worm

Sympathy pup

Nah!

I'm just gonna be me
Deep breathing and
Fingers crossed; let's see

Even In the crowd
Our eyes met
And the world started spinning
Sweaty armpits
Frozen fingers
Quivering like autumn leaf
I stood before her dumb struck

A gesture asking me to sit down
Lights off – black out
The next thing I remember
What a start!
Perfect
Waking up to see the
Attractive face hovering
Over me….
Man! I'm truly deeply madly
Scared I was

# Web of knowledge

Tied in shackles
Solid chains of iron rods
Brutally tortured
Dark deep dungeons
Thrown away to be lost
Captivated
Almost murdered
No life left
No hopes
Imprisoned
In my own mind

# Reflections of a sunset

Sitting at the river bank

Watching the slowly floating plank…

Soft wind blows forming waves

Fallen leaves fly showing paves

Grey sky all,

Yellow leave fall

Hand in hand we walked the way

There at the river bank our hearts lay

Lying under the evening sky

All I could see was his eye

Those lovely black pools of love

And the clouds gliding above….!

# Lassi in the drizzle

There are so many things I never told you
So many things you never asked
So many things I hide from you
So many times I wear masks

I just don't know how to tell you
I don't know from where to start
So much is that my love for you
I find it too small is my heart

I am so blank and so frank
I want to tell you, my love, my life
How much I love you
I fear you won't believe me

For the truth lies deep within
My heart keeps quietly screaming
I never thought that I'd lose my mind
And that I could control this

I really never meant the words I said
And for it I'm heavily paid

I know I'm a jerk, I'm a fool a pain in the neck
Would I ever become the girl I craved?

You are the perfect boy, the perfect man
But look at me, where I am?
I have no other words to say only
That I love you very badly and madly

And that I'm this crazy, over possessive fool
Who loved you is loving you and will forever
Keep on loving you unlimited without any rule
More, still more, now and forever

# Moist mornings and dew over the grass

No matter what
I love you!
One look
One smile
One sorry
I'm all yours
I always was
But again
Falling in love
With you!
Your name
Always at my lips
Your smile
Apple of my eye
Your touch
Million dollar feel
You smell
So delicious
Over and over again
Loving again
Is what I want

To do

So please

Love me back

True and too!

# Ten to three

A place unknown
A task grave
To reach destination
Confound

I remember
Remembered well
How you lead the
Way before

How we went
Singing aloud
Good songs old
Smiling all along

Does it mean,
You are perfect
For me?
Or I'm just lured!

When you knocked at my door
Then came the downpour

The abandoned room
High hopes of …
Yet it all ended
In a dreamy way

The million dollor
Hug and warmth
Love and care
So fatherly

The splendid walk
In sun fields
Sweater shades
Worthy blades

Fantasy alive
Love left lose
On a bridge
Free highway

Two terrific hours
Of just ecstasy
Peace supreme
Love divine

So pure, so naïve

So delicate, so sure
So serene, so simple
So much like you!

Cuddled up
In your arms
All safe and secure
I feel amazing
When you smile
Kiss my forehead
Caressing my eyelids
I feel cloud nine

Trance, romance
At a glance!

# Dreamless thought

Lives here
are complex
Full of pretense
Hypocrisy, malice
Though boasted to be
Simple and pure
Status symbols
Egos, reputations;
Weigh heavier
Than love
Love, which
Does not exist
Never prevailed
All gone and
Washed in drain
Along with
Their soul!

# Dead silence

When loneliness
Gathers it's army
When soul
Feels confinement
In it's own body
When heart
Screams a silent cry
In the over crowded
World
And yet no body moved
No one uttered a word
There lays
Cold and naked
The blue breathless body
Mouse eaten
Moth trodden
Maggots mansion
How shall thou
Rest in peace
Now?

# Strange songs

I've known you
For years
My unknown friend
Was it really you?
Oh dear
Don't pretend!

Do you hear it
This strange song
That we sing
When we are around
Around each other
In crowds?

For when alone
We are oceans apart
Ice-cold eyes
Nothing to talk about
The definite distance
But when there are
Million eyes

Set on us – staring
Judging our every
Single movement..
We start singing
The strange song!

You hold my hand
Longer than expected
Longer than usual
Longer than needed
Just to welcome me
Or bid me farewell

Finding reasons to
Hold my hand
Lingering around
Obviously, blankly

Holding mine in
Both your hands
Warm and strong
Looking straight
Into my eyes
As if ripping my off..
Making sure I
Notice your pupils dilate!

Your nothing whispers

Just to smell my hair
Or feel my neck at
Your tip

Raising queries and questions
In every corner possible
Strange song you sing

It's a duet that we sing
I know
For I too
Long for those crowded
Night cool and secluded
Hoping our song goes
Unheard in noise
My eyes search
Only for your approval
Of my looks and attire
I love the current
That flows by when
Our shoulders touch
Accidently of course!
Or when my little
Fingers touches yours…
Your partner in crime
I sing the song too
The gentle whispers

Of how good we look
Your soft murmuring
"Gorgeous today"
I smile and you say
I'm very beautiful today
You look
Some strange song
Indeed!